Poems about Creation

Rachael Gardner

Presentation by *BookLeaf Publishing*

Web: www.bookleafpub.com

E-mail: info@bookleafpub.com

ISBN: 9789360945251

First edition 2024

This book is for my children, Edmund and Adam, and for my nieces and nephews: Jason, Michael, David Nicholas, Isaac, Louis, Samantha, David Michael, Mackenzie, Joey, James, Kaylee, Elliana, Aidan, Gracie, Savannah, Christian, Liana, Juliette, and Isaak.

ACKNOWLEDGEMENT

I would like to thank Pastor Ed Marcelle, who taught me to love the story of Creation. Because of your labor, I am a better disciple of Jesus Christ.

PREFACE

Jesus said, "You search the Scriptures because you think that in them you have eternal life; and it is they that bear witness about me" (John 5:39, ESV taken from the YouVersion app). This book is my attempt to demonstrate how the Creation story demonstrates the character and the heart of God in a way that even little children can understand. I hope that it becomes something parents will read to their children before bed, and I pray that those children grow up knowing that our God is good, and faithful, and loves them very much.

On beginnings

Just for starters, God created.
Here's a title so you know
It was OUR God who created
Heavens above and earth below.

It was OUR God who has done it
Not the gods of other lands
Who spoke worlds into existence
And who made us with his hands.

'Twas OUR God who hovered over
Formless earth and empty space,
And who breathed his life into it--
Shined his glory in this place.

In the things he has created
OUR God has clearly shown
Endless power and sacred beauty;
He has made HIS nature known.

So we thank OUR God and honor him;
To him we lift our eyes.
If you do this, little children,
Then OUR God will make you wise.

The Pattern

There's a pattern you should notice:
God has said, and it was so.
This applies to us today
Just as much as long ago.

What God says will surely happen;
All his purposes will be.
All he does will bring him glory
And bring joy to you and me.

Thus another pattern emerges:
"And God saw that it was good."
He is pleased with his creation
This is what we can conclude.

Then the evening and the morning--
Every day is a new day.
It's a pattern we can trust
God's faithfulness is on display.

The commander of the cosmos
In his wisdom and his might
Has created laws of nature,
And they prove him to be right.

(So) When you see the world around you,
And its lessons help you grow
Note that it is by God's wisdom,
Not by chance that it is so.

Light, the First Day

And God said, "Let there be light,"
And there was light and it was good.
And the light he separated from the darkness
As it should

To make the evening and the morning--
Something different in their role.
In our finite human existence,
These two halves must make a whole.

But this light that God created
Independent of the sun
Shows that is by God's power
And his word that it is done.

When God says, "Let there be light,"
There will be light forevermore
Darkness will not overcome it
For the Faithful makes it sure.

Space, the Second Day

Just as God had separated
Light and Darkness to their place,
He then separated water
For environment and space.

Mind you, heaven and space were empty--
A blank canvas for his art.
Possibilities were endless!
What would come from God's great heart?

But he paused there for his pleasure;
He made nothing else that day
He made only separation
In his high and priestly way.

There is order. There is purpose
To this glorious, humble start
For it shows that God is holy--
What is HIS is set apart.

Land and Seas, the Third Day

Then God gathered under heaven
All its water into seas,
And he said, "Let the dry land appear,"
And with it he was pleased.

Thus the backdrop was completed;
All the places had been made.
These containers for reflection
That his glory be displayed.

These materials held nourishment
For life still yet to be,
So God filled the land with color--
Vegetation on day three.

Seed-bearers

Then the Word of God commanded
That the earth sprout plants and trees
With its reproductive power
Holding, each of them, a seed.

And the earth, of course, obeyed;
It was obligated so.
Earth grew plants and plants had seeds
And from seeds new plants would grow.

But in order to accomplish this
The seeds fell to the ground
And in dead earth, and in dying seed,
Was new life to be found.

Plants make plants according to their kind,
My children, take great care
For the harvest that you reap depends
On what is planted there.

Sun, Moon, and Stars, the Fourth Day

Then God delegated power
Thus to govern night and day:
He ordained the sun and moon
To maintain order in this way.

Greater light to rule the daytime,
Shine on earth and make things grow.
Lesser lights to rule the nighttime,
Causing tides to ebb and flow.

Through them God made separation
Times and seasons, days and years;
And each season serves its purpose
'til a new season appears.

In these seasons, grass may wither
Stars may from their stations fall;
But God's Word remains forever--
Stands in contrast to it all.

So remember, little children,
Though the daylight has its end,
That the night won't last forever;
Only God is permanent.

Fish and Birds, the Fifth Day

Then God spoke into the water
And he spoke into the sky
To create the great sea creatures
And the winged birds that fly.

Then he blessed them with this blessing,
"Be fruitful and multiply."
And they did, for God had spoken,
Produce offspring of their kind.

In deepest depths and highest heights,
There lives a testament
That for each creature God provides
And makes himself present.

Land Animals, the Sixth Day

Then God spoke to earth again
That it bring forth new kinds of life
Beasts and cattle and the creeping things
According to their kind.

Thus God made them with his words
As he had done each day before,
But he was not done creating;
In his heart was something more.

(But what he did next was quite unexpected...)

The Creation of Humanity

Then our God said something different--
Something more than "Let there be..."
"Let us make" them in our image
And give them authority.

Let the humans rule the fish
And rule the creatures of the sky,
And all that wanders on the earth
Must to their word comply.

God formed the first man out of dust
And in his nostrils blew;
The Holy Spirit raised him up
And made him something new.

To show the man's dominion
God put creatures in his way,
And he told Adam to name them
Just to see what he would say.

But in naming all the animals
A problem became known
For all had passed him two by two
But Adam was alone.

And so again God said what no one
Could anticipate:
He called "Not good" the thing that his own
hands
And breath had made.

So he planned to make a helper
For strategic partnership;
He put the man to sleep
And removed from him his rib.

Adam Suffers for his Bride

Now God had formed out of the ground
The beasts and all the birds
And all Creation until Adam
Came from just his words.

And breath that God breathed into man
Made him a living soul
Now wounds from God would break him
So that he could be made whole.

God caused the man to fall asleep
And pierced him in his side;
Around the bone removed from him
God built for him his bride.

Then Adam, rising from his sleep
Like rising from the dead
Received his bride unto himself
And this is what he said:

"She is bone of my bones
And her flesh is of my flesh!"
So he called his partner "Woman,"
And they both in nakedness

Were unashamed for now reflected
In their unity
The image of our God they were
As they were meant to be.

And God said it was very good
He bid them rule and reign
And fill the earth and cultivate
The glory of his name.

God gave us life and meaning,
Purpose for the things we do
For he made us to be like him
And we are creators, too.

God Rests, the Seventh Day

After six days of creating
All the heavens and the earth
And the seas and all that swarm in it
The sky and all its birds

All the plants and all the trees
All of the land and creatures, too,
And the humans in his image
Who, like him, would earth subdue

God rested from his labor
Celebrated all his feats
For the earth and heav'n
And all that dwell within them was complete.

And he called the Sabbath holy
For himself did separate it
For it was the day he rested
From the works he had created.

The Fall

Now, the serpent--he was crafty
And he called the woman out
From the safety of her marriage
And he put God's words in doubt.

So the woman was deceived
And did not accurately transmit
What the law that God had given
Did certainly forbid.

Then she sinned and called her husband
And he listened and complied
And on the day the first man sinned
All flesh in Adam died.

Then they both saw they were naked
And from God's presence hid
And God cried to them, "Where are you?"
For to him, they were now dead.

But they told God of their nakedness
And that they were afraid.
Then they took turns pointing fingers
As to why they disobeyed.

So first, God cursed the serpent
And with that he guaranteed
The serpent lose the war between him
And the woman and her seed.

Then he multiplied the sorrow
Of the woman giving birth
And set her against her husband
And subordinated her.

And to Adam he said this:
"Because you listened to your wife..."
You will work in pain and eat in pain
For all of your long life.

And to dust you shall return
For it was from the dust you came.
Then God shed the blood of animals
To cover up their shame.

Then God cast them from the garden
Guarded it with flaming sword
And they died in separation
From the glory of the Lord.

But they died believing promises
That there would be a child
Who would see their sin defeated
And their glory reconciled.

Why I Tell This Story

This may all seem quite familiar
You may question very well
Why I've gone through all the pains
Of this old story to retell.

But I love to tell this story,
And this is the reason why:
Because all that's in the Scripture
Does of Jesus testify.

If you understand Creation,
You will know that it is true
That the story of Redemption
Has been hidden in it, too.

Have you missed it?
Let's review...

Jesus, the Creator and the Light

In the beginning was the Word
He was with God, and was God.
And he made all that was made,
And without him there was naught.

In him was life, and life was that
Which lights the hearts of men;
So the light that he created
Also testifies of him.

For the Light shines in the darkness
And will not be overcome
And his word will stand forever
All his purpose will be done.

Jesus, Our Great High Priest

When we think of separation
Of the water from the space
We remember Jesus passed through heav'n
To come into this place.

For the Word became flesh just like us
Was tempted yet was without sin
Was baptized for repentance
And calls us to enter in.

So he helps us when we're tempted,
Makes us perfect as we suffer,
Brings us with him into glory,
Unashamed to call us brothers.

Jesus is our Great High Priest
Who through his death delivered us;
He's the founder of salvation
And in him we put our trust.

Jesus, the Chosen Seed

When we think of how God separated
Water from dry earth,
Its growing plants with fruit and seeds
Reminds us of childbirth.

It reminds us of the promise giv'n the serpent
With his curse:
A seed of woman would crush his head
--And Jesus was the first!

For as in Adam all men died
Christ, too, died in our place
And led us through the water
Out of slavery into grace.

He has spoken to the dry and empty
Land that was our hearts
Has made it sprout with new life
And set us, for him, apart.

So Jesus is the chosen seed
The promised son of Eve
Has conquered death, made us alive
In this we must believe.

Jesus, the Lord of the Harvest

The delegated rule of sun and moon
O'er day and night
Reminds us all authority
Is given Jesus Christ.

Who calls us to a new day
A new year of the Lord
A new season of the harvest
As directed by his word.

He said, "Go and make disciples"--
Every race and tongue must know
Of the things that I have taught you;
I am with you as you go.

Ask of me and I will send forth
Workers with you, too
For the fields are ripe with harvest
But the laborers are few.

Redeem the time, for seasons
Can be relatively short
And there will be a day
When sun and moon will be no more.

Jesus, the Head of the Body

We recall that God made Adam
And then built from him his wife;
This reminds us of the new Adam
Our Savior, Jesus Christ.

He left his father's throne above
To be with us one flesh
Was crucified, was dead, was raised
To raise in righteousness

A bride, who borne of suffering
Became bone of his bone
A holy city built around
Jesus, the Cornerstone.

And now we are Christ's body
Doing works he has prepared
We're building up and being built
With Jesus as our Head.

Rest for God's People

When we think about the Sabbath--
How it marked God's work complete
We remember what our Savior said,
The words he did repeat:

"It is finished" were his final words
Upon the cross that eve
For he fulfilled all of the Law
For those who would believe.

In this he has commanded us
To rest from our dead works
To rest in him whose very word
Upholds the universe.

For nothing we can do
Could add to us the righteousness
That Christ has given freely;
Do not put him to the test.

But trust him and obey him
In the work he calls complete
And the works you do will become jewels
You cast at Jesus' feet.

God is Faithful

The lesson of this story
Is that God is who we trust.
He has made us; He preserves us;
He redeemed and called us just.

And his word does not go out
Unless it does what he intends
And he works all things together
To accomplish this one end:

Those he calls, he calls "Not guilty,"
He will not be called a liar
He produces good in us
'Til we are gold refined by fire.

'Til we fully are transformed
Into his image radiant
We can put our hope in Jesus
And of this be confident:

He won't leave his work unfinished;
He will always see it through.
We can trust it to be sure that
What he says is what he'll do.